From Whence

poems

from Whence

Michael Chitwood

LOUISIANA STATE UNIVERSITY PRESS
BATON ROUGE

Published by Louisiana State University Press

Manufactured in the United States of America

An LSU Press Paperback Original
First printing

Designer: Michelle A. Garrod
Typefaces: Warnock Pro, Typewriter
Printer and binder: Edwards Brothers, Inc.

Thanks to the following magazines, their editors, and their readers, in which these poems first appeared: *Carolina Quarterly,* "Out Here" (1998); *Christian Century,* "Acolyte"(1999); *Field,* "At the Wilco with Some Founding Fathers," "From Whence," "Threshold" (all 2001), "His Gratitude," "Oscillating Fan" (both 2000); *JAMA,* "The Puzzles" (1999); *Mudfish,* "Correspondence" (No. 10); *New Republic,* "Virginia History" (2001); *Ohio Review,* "The Seasons Come and the Seasons Keep Coming" (No. 54); *Oxford American,* "Revival" (2000); *Poetry,* "Basement Barber" (1993), "Chalk" (1997), "Duty and History" (1998), "Morning Walk, Holden Beach" (2002); *Quarterly West,* "Baptist" (2000); *Slate,* "The Small-Town Voice of God"; *Southern Review,* "Grammar," "Telling It" (both 2003); *The Sun,* "Talc like Dust" (1997); *Tar River Poetry,* "Easy Street, Continental Homes, Luck, the Destination of Southern Conversation, and Dust" (1995); *Threepenny Review,* "Assistant" (1993), "The Wedding at Cana" (1998), "Science or History, I Forget Which" (1999), "Division" (2002); *TriQuarterly,* "The Inheritance: A Lamentation" (No. 103), "The One Day," "Men Throwing Bricks" (both No. 114); *Virginia Quarterly Review,* "Digging," "Skinning" (both 2002).

The author would like to thank Michael McFee, Alan Shapiro, Danny Anderson, and Gary Bolt for generous support and much help with the poems.

Library of Congress Cataloging-in-Publication Data

Chitwood, Michael.
From whence : poems / Michael Chitwood.
p. cm.
ISBN: 978-0-8071-3224-1 (pbk. : alk. paper)
I. Title

PS3553.H535F76 2007
811'54—dc22

2006018259

The paper in this book meets the guidelines for permanence and durability of the Committee on Production Guidelines for Book Longevity of the Council on Library Resources. ♾

For Jean,
from whence

I lift up my eyes to the hills.
From whence does my help come?
—PSALM 121

Contents

Threshold

Your Shade on Your Right Hand

Digging

Threshold

Chalk

Cartridge of thought,
stick of screech

in our unlearned pinch.
Arithmetic's cigarette,

the answers vanishing
in the giggle at our backs.

Mistakes rub off
white on our fingers.

This dusty little bone
shows our ignorance

as we tap
a meaningless code

on the powdered tray.
Hands are being raised.

But here is praise,
the soft applause

of the erasers
as we beat the answers

out of them.
Pythagoras, Cortés,

blue of the earthworm's gut,
red-letter dates,

all drift from us
and our standing ovation

to another chance,
a new day's clean slate.

The Garden

We were chosen,
a girl and a boy,
to wind our way through the woods
to the abandoned house
just off school property

where, every spring, the jonquils volunteered.
Someone—a woman now dead?—started
the first bed, but now,
everywhere, dozens, the yellow lantern heads.

They were the models, pistil and stamen,
we would dissect.
We needed twenty-eight.
One for each student's dull scalpel.

What I remember
is the way she squatted,
her legs tucked, the dark beneath her skirt,
her blouse, her breast,
the quick scissors and her hand's bouquet.

Acolyte

One of the smokers,
Tom Via or Franklin Furrow,
would thumb his lighter open
and pop the flame to the waxen wick,
then he'd click it shut, hike up his choir robe
and tuck the potent silver box back against his thigh.
I held God's stick, fingering the trigger
that fed the wick to Jesus, light of the world.
Not too much, it would make smoke and risk
scorching the cross when I honored it.
Too little and even the breeze
of my slow pace would snuff it.
Could I kill God?
I loved the thing's economy,
double-headed, the flame and the silent bell
for smothering the flame.
All week it hung beneath the preacher's robe
behind the door to the choir loft.
It rattled with every entrance and waited
to be ignited by the instrument of a man's death.
All Sunday afternoon,
I could taste its brass on my hands.

The Drawing

She used the exotic chalks
from her lower desk drawer,
pink, yellow, blue. A flower
bloomed in the blackboard dust,

a flower from the wildest spring.
Its blossom lured names
like scent-crazed bees—pistil,
stamen, anther, petal.

The stigma was blue. Her hands,
fluted and white as Easter lilies,
were smeared with touching up
the drawing. She smudged for depth.

And later, when the labels
were erased for the test,
the arrows flew at the blossom
as in a sketch on a cave wall.

Could we remember what was what?
The blue rod, the pink opening?
Would the names let us understand?
The barbed sticks jabbed but never struck.

Music Lesson

His voice like an air wrench,
he sat at the kitchen table
still greasy from some repair,
and, shoeless, talked to his boys

while I finished my lesson.
The white keys were teeth,
slightly yellowed like his.
A pot simmered on the stove.

His name was red on his shirt,
mine block print on the book
I held, a shield at my chest,
to walk by. His white feet,

toes long it seemed as my fingers
that could not learn the waltz,
were animals beneath his chair.
I expected them to snap or snarl.

He looked up to ask me
what meat there would be
and she answered over my head.
“Pork chop.” I went by and out,

my hands hot with clutching.
Those feet, hairy on top,
could kick a tire from its rim,
push loose a rusty lug.

Those feet under covers could
nuzzle and school with hers.
It was getting dark and damp.
The chained dog started to bark.

Organist

It seemed it took all of her
to play it. Her smooth hands worked
the double keyboard, her shoulders
rolled under the robe when she reached
to the stops, oboe, lute, or harp.
She'd unsnap the robe, bottom up,
and spread it back over the bench
to give her legs the freedom they needed.
Only I could see her feet.
She'd taken off her shoes
to feel the low-register pedals
with the private dark toe of her Sunday hose.
Through "Holy, Holy, Holy" and "I Love
Thy Kingdom, Lord" I was acolyte
to her organ's hum. The Word,
as her hymns swelled, became flesh.

Duty and History

My father is polishing his wingtips,
left hand up to the wrist
in his right shoe, right hand
wielding the brush, *ush fluff,*
like the flutter of a dove.

There's a whole congregation
inside the green Zenith
on the counter in the kitchen
where he is polishing his wingtips.
It's the Hubbard Sheet Metal Works'
"Little Country Church," and Ralph Stanley
is singing "On the Wings of a Dove."
My father hums along,
his left hand up to the wrist in the left shoe.

Now the shoes are standing
on the mat of newspaper
my father has spread on the kitchen floor.
They gleam like caskets
on the pictures and headlines of Vietnam.
The Sunday morning light
is living up to its name on their black hides.
It's as though no one is standing at attention
on old news, already forgotten,
already left for something else

like these four doves I notice in the dogwood
just off the porch where I am remembering
those empty shoes, those gleaming empty shoes,
strict in their attitude on top of some sad history.

The proper name is Mourning Dove.
Four of them in the dogwood.

Revival

". . . and ever see them again,
who would it be, Grandma? A wife?
Your father?
All the loved ones you knew in this life?
If you are to see them
you must die this night and be born again,
washed in the blood that was shed for you."
The old furnace knocked and moaned
as if all the damned below
were clamoring for our company.
"Will you see them again? Will you take them
once more to your bosom?"
A wasp, resurrected by the furnace heat,
tapped the stained glass.
And when it was over,
we found it was snowing, silent and strangely light.
Each flake, each one individual we knew,
disappeared into all the others
and made a place for the moonlight to rest.

Science or History, I Forget Which

A certain portion of dirt—
is this like Archimedes' discovery
when he lowered himself
into his bath?—
would not fit back into the graves.

They piled it all together,
a mound of . . . what was it,
specific gravity, volume, net weight?
I've forgotten the lesson.

But when it rained
we marched barefoot on it.
This was the benefit of living
so near a graveyard.
The wet red clay clung to our soles.

Correspondence

We're learning the six parts of a letter. Sender's address, date, address of recipient, greeting or salutation, body of the letter, the closing.

"Who are we writing to?" John Thurman wants to know.

"That's not important," Miss Scott says.

"It's not?" John asks. He rubs his hand over his head. "How will we know what to say?"

"This is about the form a letter takes," Miss Scott explains.

Here's the body of the letter. It's been laid out on the kitchen table. I've heard my grandmother describe this. It was in a letter from her sister in Virginia. The body on the table. All the ladies gathered to wash it. It's pale, almost blue like milk after the cream has risen.

"We did not know what to say."

Grammar

"Like a girl's skirt,
your essay should be long enough
to cover the subject
but short enough to make it interesting,"
Miss Knox would say,
her own skirt just barely covering
the subject, the object
of all our young verbs, boys
at the riotous threshold of manhood.
When her sentences climbed the scaffolding
of the diagram, dismantling into parts,
we ached with the rise
of that hemline.
She left a wake in the hallway,
waft of Chanel and gazes dragged along
like snagged anchor lines.
Sentences came apart, parts of speech
sticking in our throats when she'd hike herself
to sit on her desk top for the grammar quiz.
She must have known
we called her Fort Knox
for her strict, no-guff-allowed classroom.
Her paddle was nearly jaunty,
leaning in the corner like a street-corner tough.
Mouth off or clown the lesson
and a boy would have to grab his ankles
and she behind
with both hands gripping the paddle
would take a legs-spread stance and swing.
The air, even when she stopped, would sing.
We had everything to learn,
everything between noun and verb.

Assistant

"Come down here,"
he said at the bottom

of the basement steps.
Dank, musky as turned dirt,

it held everything that died
in our lives,

old encyclopedias, lame chairs,
coats collapsed in a heap,

a good place to pout
or hide out for the panic

long disappearances
caused upstairs.

Was he excited or afraid?
"Hold this with both hands."

He wrapped the itchy rope
around my wrists.

"No matter what,
don't touch me."

Mother's footsteps
worried overhead.

The World Books hid
under their downy mold.

He opened the gray box
behind the water heater.

The rope was heavy
as the science-show snake.

He reached into the live box.
Would I be enough,

if the current grabbed,
to help him let go?

Basement Barber

Here were said the words men say.
The oil stove winked its slit black eye;
it knew they did not have their way.

A whitetail made for the edge of the page.
Vitalis came before the talc.
My father's dark hair began to fade.

Barrelhead Thurman palmed my scalp,
knuckled my ear when he was done
just to hear a little boy yelp.

They rode, hats off, through years of lies
on bus seats the county junked,
out-fished, out-hunted the ones who'd died.

My father's dark hair began to fade.
The oil stove winked its slit black eye.
It knew he did not have his way.

The dead grow long and beautiful hair.
They have said what they had to say
to stir that basement's damp, sweet air.

Division

Inside the shed, he'd rigged
an oil drip into the barrel stove
so that the used sludge from his trucks
burned with split hickory while he
passed the winter piecing together furniture.
Just a sideline, he'd say, aiming
down a board to judge it in or out of true.
"It fills in the down months and tacks
some cash on the end of the year."

In those same white weeks at school
I learned division. First, you made a lean-to
for the big number to go under. The little
number waited outside. You could add on
as many zeros as you wanted.
The answer appeared on the roof.
December and January passed into February
and a whole bedroom suite came together.
On the roof, the smoke swirled into *0*s and *8*s.

The Round, Turning World

It was all women
and children.
This was 1965.

A few coughed
or slumped against
their mothers.

The rest of us
tucked our hands
under our knees

and swung our feet
above the floor.
It was just a check-up.

You spoke your name
through the hole
in the glass.

When someone was called
they went behind a wall
Mom said was glass brick.

They wavered
like the vapor
off a hot road.

Then he came in.
He'd been working
next door

and was holding up
his hand and blood
ran into his sleeve.

His crushed fingers
trembled and a nurse
ran. She ran

with him,
her hand on his back,
so quick behind

the wall
they evaporated,
but his soles

had left
five-sided molds
of mud

like tiny cookies
on the floor
and the blood,

his black stubble,
her small hand,
her quick trot,

the swish of her white
hose, made the room
lurch sideways,

I felt it move
and wanted
to pick up

one of the
mud cookies
and eat it.

Threshold

The car that knocked the deer to the roadside
is long gone. Maybe there's gray-brown bristle still stuck
to the fender, maybe a dent in the quarter panel.
This time of year they don't decay so much as deflate,
the rawhide bag leaking until it's flat,
the hair matted and sodden with cinder-pocked snow.
Come spring, there'll be a scar in the shoulder grass
where the doe sagged into a tattered rug,
welcome mat at the random threshold of the next world.
The pond is holding up the stone a boy threw.
He won't be here to notice, he may no longer be a child,
when the ice softens just enough for the rock
to ease through and plunge to the pond's dark bottom.

Your Shade on Your Right Hand

The Puzzles

They spent afternoons healing landscapes,
filling in a mountainside in only two hours.
They reunited still lives,
the pear back with its grapes and vase.
And then her cells crowded into the picture.

It was her system he loved,
her practical philosophy.
First, all the pieces turned up
so you could see what you had,
even if it was only a scrap of yellow.
Then the border,
the tell-tale straight edge making it easy,
why not make it easy?
Then the heart of the matter,
castle, boat dock, whatever.
Finally the most difficult,
the sky, the water, the field,
the vague blue-green that held it together.

Best was the missing piece—
lost, never included?—
always one he wouldn't know about
until the sky's odd-shaped little completion
couldn't be found.

Mass-produced, sentimental,
they're a gallery around the basement pool table,
varnished but never finished.
He's sure now she hid it.

His Gratitude

Women still wed to the living bring casseroles in disposable tins.
When he's finished, he puts them down for the dog
whose licking rattles the tin across the hardwood.
It's a sound like a barn roof when the barn has burned
and the wind comes for the rusted remains, like children
jumping on the hood of a junked car, like static
when the station's gone but the volume's still high.
It is everything he has to say, the work of the tongue
pushing the container across the floor for its next-to-nothings.

Luke's Mom

She is standing outside the Eckerd,
the neat close-cropped gray hair, a fleecy black coat,
are those sweat pants? and black Reeboks.
It's been, what, five or six years since she died?
She seems to be waiting for someone to pick her up
and I almost ask if Luke is coming by.
Does he know you're in town, I mean, that you're back?
I very nearly say. She has that patient, contented
expression that I remember from the last years when she
seemed so happy, even working at the dumpy department store.
Luke and I would go by and she'd be sighing at the desperate
lives of the young employees and offering mild advice,
not the kind she could have handed out, given
the shit she'd been through, all the dramas
Luke recounted to me in our dorm room when study stalled
and it was late and quiet and he would tell
about the time he talked her out of using the razor,
her sitting on the edge of the tub, a wrist turned up
and him catching her, how calmly he talked even though he
was only about 12 or 13, he couldn't remember.
Scene after scene with his dad, the sloppy punches, the screams.
It was more like he was thinking out loud about a play
he was reading for a Lit class, trying to understand
if there was a hero and if it was the mother.
I know it's not her, of course, but this woman is a twin,
great job by the casting director down to the relaxed
way she holds her mouth as if she's about to smile.
I want to tell her that I'm so glad she's here
because I've always wanted to ask her, for Luke's sake
and now I know mine too, how she did it.
How did you survive?
But suddenly her ride arrives, a big sedan
with out-of-state plates, and she is gone.

Praise

Physical therapists have opened a clinic in the office next to mine. This morning one of them is treating a cystic fibrosis patient. The patient lies face down on a table, and the therapist slaps up and down the back with open hands. It loosens the mucus building up in the lungs. Through the wall, it sounds like one person giving a long, determined standing ovation.

Finally, I've listened long enough and go out for a walk. The church across the street has just reseeded its lawn, and the caretaker is trying to shoo away pigeons that are feeding in the straw.

"Get! Get!" he shouts, and claps his hands.

The pigeons rise in unison and swirl away with a sound like gloved applause.

The One Day

We were behind on the job
so we waited out the rain in the pickup.
Because the backhoe would mire
he shouldered the four-foot pipe joints
and brought them to us in the ditch.
The red mud clutched and tugged at his boots
and Bill laughed at his "Swan Lake"
as he fought through, lurching and staggering
when the mud would suddenly let go.
But he kept them coming, lugging the red joints
to us and then slogging back for another
while we slid on the gasket and fit the pipes together.
You can see how, pushing like that, he wound up,
two years later, with the tiny plastic piping of IVs
feeding into both arms and the three drainage tubes
snaking from under the patch on his chest.
His skin was a shade away from being same as the sheet
when I saw him in the ICU,
and he couldn't have lifted the drinking straw
on the bedside tray.
But that one day he brought two hundred yards of pipe
and even the red earth couldn't stop him.

Telling It

For instance, my mother's uncle
who showed up at my aunt and uncle's
one afternoon. He was drunk; he was nearly
always drunk when he wasn't at work.
There was another man with him,
also drunk. They were angry
or at least they had been angry
when they hatched their plan
which was that they would get my uncle
to drive them around while they got
in the back seat and had a fight.
Oh, the beautiful logic of alcohol.
They had negotiated county roads
and managed one-lane bridges
and remembered all the correct turns
and come to my uncle's house
and when he asked them why
they were going to fight they
roared and stumbled around
and admitted that now they couldn't
remember, but needed to fight anyway
they were sure of that. They're both
dead now, at least my mother's uncle
is and the other one too, I imagine;
anyone who would get that drunk
and form such a totally American plan—
to fight in a driven car, the strange reverse
of making love in a parked one—
must be dead. And yet it adheres,
that story, that ridiculous idea.
It's told and implicates us all,
my mother, my uncle, me, them,
our telling it making them live again,
making us a little dead in our passing it on
for its sad grand stupidity, anger,

forgetfulness, and laughter
that will in turn pass on again
because it is such a good story
when the dead want to fight.

The Inheritance: A Lamentation

Here it is at last, the indistinguishable thing.
Schooled, well read in grief,
even in gnashing and wailing, the women driven weeping
    before the chariots,
and I do not even cough out a dry cry—

just a phrase is all—a goddamn phrase, silent and repeating
in my inner voice, you know the voice you hear,
though *hear* isn't the right word
since it's never spoken,
but the voice that says your words
when you are silently planning what to say.

Look how far off the subject I've already gotten.

I want to blame this on heredity.
It's a Hall trait—my mother's people.
Sarcastic, more than one genuinely funny
in a jerk-your-pants-down-and-embarrass-you-in-front-of-everyone
    kind of way,
but all strangely quiet in calamity.

For example—
see even in the midst of what began with weeping
I can say "For example"—
there was the time I was driving toward them, grandmother just dead.
I was ready to be born into family sadness,
Mother, the aunts, crying, I imagined,
when I emerged from my car.
They sat on the front porch.
"Here, Michael, have a seat," Mom said.

And suddenly now I'm seated beside grief
and everything in the room is equal,
the gray and black ultrasound screen
with its masses and blobs like a high-pressure weather pattern,

a greeting card propped open on the desk,
it must be from the technician's husband,
I can read *ove you, honey* in a jerky cursive,
the tube of gel the tech slathered on the wand,
my wife weeping,
the first time I've heard genuine, driven-before-the-chariots weeping.

It was a Hall response.
The emotional fuse blows,
I never knew it came with a distracting phrase,
and we're left silent and dark.
The technician's diploma is elegantly framed.
It says, I'm sure,
the print is too small for me to read,
she is qualified.
She knows a dead child when she sees one.

When I would ask him a question
on the way to a job site,
my uncle, Mother's younger brother, would turn his ruined eye,
blinded when a piece of steel flew from a struck survey spike,
so I could see it
and say, "You writin' a book?"
Once I got smart-mouthed enough to answer, "Yeah."
"Well, kiss my ass and make it a love story."

I squeeze Jean's hand,
try to press enough to comfort her.
The technician wipes the gel from the wand,
and then from where she had smeared Jean's abdomen.
The phrase, ridiculous, surreal, inappropriate,
repeats aloud in my head.
But it is unheard in this room
with the blue pocketbook under the desk.
The ultrasound pipes and squeaks.
When a piece of heavy equipment broke down,

my uncle, Flukie is his nickname,
would emit a high-pitched, feedback-type shrill
before he would pour out the most eloquent, well-delivered
oration of cussing I, to this day, have ever heard.
It was inspired, a regular lamentation.

Hard to believe a man so gifted distrusted, even openly disdained,
anyone who made a living with words,
salesmen, reporters, DJs, preachers,
especially preachers.
But listen to him,
on an August day, in a rage at a backhoe,
shaking a socket wrench over his head and shouting,
"I would just as soon carve a wooden bill
and go peck shit with the ducks
as try to make a living with this goddamn yellow motherfucker."

The ample shade of maples.
I squeeze Jean's hand.
The technician balls up the coarse paper wipes.
The ample shade of maples.

"Wish in one hand
and shit in the other.
See which one fills up faster,"
Flukie would say
when I wanted what wasn't
or what was to be wasn't.

My child that was, now wasn't
and in my hand I hold a hand
so full of grief, yes it even fills her hand,
that it cannot be touched
even as I clutch it.

The ample shade of maples.
The ample shade of maples.
The tech peels off her skin-tight gloves

and tosses them, inside out,
into an orange plastic trash can.
She's done with us.

What will we do for the rest of the day?
Where will we go?
What will my job be?

Flukie turned slightly
so I could see his unseeing
bad black eye, grinned, took pity
and didn't ask this time if I was writing a book
which I was, as we all are, in memory,
a love story.

Good Heart

She wishes she had never gone into research. Now she knows the bouts of intense sadness that walk through her life—everything bombed out and vacant—are just chemical. The curious pang she feels when she sees the doctors in their white coats coming down the sidewalk returning from rounds was pleasantly unexplainable before. Now, something about the white jackets strobing off the grass causes a release . . . she doesn't want to know anymore.

She knows even joy moves through the body ignorant as water rising in the stalk of a chrysanthemum.

Oh, these wooden racks, their vials and graduated cylinders.

It is a good job and valuable work, she knows, but there was a nice routine to the old job in the surgery suite. Each morning, the saw for the sternum, spreading the rib cage, the frightened bird inside.

Skinning

How many times did I hold them up for him
and watch how easily something that had lived
comes apart? In each hand I clutched
an unlucky foot and splayed them, belly-side
to him, and he'd pinch the fur at the crotch
and with the knife point separate the fur
from the muscle and fat underneath. He'd cut
all the way around until it seemed the rabbit's
long shirt had ridden up and then with one tug
he'd pull the fur down the body and over the head
the same way you'd tug the pajamas off a child.
From being plush, they suddenly looked frail, naked,
even old though most had known only two autumns.
Then with three or four quick flicks of the knife
he took the head and always the little headless nude
swung back and struck me in the chest.
Carefully, so as not to nick a gut, he slid the knife
under the belly skin and opened the little body.
Intestines, bladder, and lungs spilled out but he would
have to pull them free, the glob in pink folds
like a sopping handkerchief dangling from his fingers.
He'd toss it over into the weeds and say a meal
for something passing in the night. In the night
when I startled out of sleep in the chair beside his bed
his bare, shrunken chest seemed so suddenly old
that again it knocked terribly against me, the dead weight.
Hold it up, he would say, higher. And I did.

Check-Up

When his platelet count tanked
and his gums began to leak blood
I wondered if this was the doctor's
warned-of "life-ending event."

But here he is, hiked up
on the clinic exam bed
in his undershirt and those green—
God, what shade is that?—

green, green, green slacks.
Only a man who has heard his death
foretold, who heard the odds
of surviving the chemo, surviving an infection,

surviving the bleeding, should it occur,
the odds of it occurring,
only such a man
should be allowed to wear such green pants.

And yet anyone could,
any schmo out for a bargain
could have taken them from the rack.
But he did and today walks away in them.

Digging

Morning Walk, Holden Beach

for Tom Andrews

Ghost moon in the upper right-hand corner
where we used to write our names—

Is it quiet there, Tom,
adrift from your drift of ashes?

I strike out towards the rising sun,
your blank blue, your murmur in surf

to my right, dunes, and salt-blasted beach fronts
to my left. I can still see

the scribblings sand crabs left
in their nightly scurry for the day's discards.

This page, like all the others, will be erased
soon, but for now there's a line or two.

The waves unscroll their best bond,
a finish like a mirror under the sandpipers.

You'd like that, I think, text as pure reflection,
no scuff of us to mar the brief recording.

There are no hills here to look to for help
though the ocean seems upgrade at the horizon.

I sing a little under my breath, as the saying goes—
old JT, Dylan, even that God-awful

song about West Virginia where your urn lies,
my honest friend, at Point Pleasant.

The sun's up now, full, and gulls yuck
at their own stand-up. I smell coffee

and turn, my back to the sun's hot yolk,
to head for home, following my shadow.

Quarters, Dimes, Nickels

You think it's only money, this change
on the bottom of municipal pools,
this silver rain that spilled from towels
and the little mesh pockets inside swimsuits?
It works loose and fishtails to the concrete bottom.
At night the dead dive for it,
their long hair undulant as seaweed,
Washingtons, Roosevelts, Jeffersons,
the dead scour the bottom like headhunters
and then it's off to the drink machines,
the snack box that advises, "Don't go around
hungry." The dead are starved,
staying under so long and the hard scissor kicks
really build an appetite and they can't forget
those crackers, those bright orange crackers
that are a color of nothing else in life or the afterlife,
the color of nothing else and the dead must have them.
Some nights it's like that—the dead ravenous,
the damp amoeba-blots of their soles on the concrete,
the smell of chlorine.

The Seasons Come and the Seasons Keep Coming

The pines are letting drift
                    their clouds of sexual dust.
It makes me cough. It makes me think
about a glass of water.

This time of year
            the pond is velvet
as though Pharaoh's whole army
has trooped by,
        the stamp causing the dirt road to lift
and resettle.

Every season has its own dust,
confection of the dry snow,
                July's talc and baby powder,
shelled corn running out of the Harvestor's hourglass.

Every season lifts and resettles
                the speck in your eye.
It makes me think about the glass
of the water.
        Look in
and you're the floating sexual dust
caught in the shimmer,
            the surface tension.

Virginia History

David Cuff, where in the fifth grade
did you get that husky voice,
that voice from a room full of smoke
and the bodies of women swaying?
"Sittin' in the mo'nin' sun,
I'll be sittin' when the evenin' comes,"
you sang to me after Mrs. Burnett
called Jefferson "the Genius of Monticello."
We were to remember that
for the Virginia history identification quiz.

Voice from a room full of smoke
and the bodies of women swaying,
you smelled of cigarettes and a woodstove
and your laugh was like the underside of a log,
damp, warm, coming apart, worked by something
from the biology textbook.

When I looked across Elich Atkins' broad backside
and broader back and saw you on defense,
grinning linebacker of the apocalypse,
I knew I would not complete the pass.
I knew I would hear that laugh
through the earhole of my nearly unscarred helmet.

What brought you back, David Cuff,
was a voice on the radio, a voice
not as freighted as I remember yours,
and after the song the talk
of black and white and black always knowing
blackness and white not living daily with the knowledge
of whiteness, not noticing, even today,
the white artists always juking the black artists
only toning it down, ha, ha, ha, ha,
the anger of the black artists, the integrity

of some white producers, the greed of white
record companies, the records,
the black records becoming white records.

David Cuff, I have to remember I once loved you.
I have to remember the chalk dust on Mrs. Burnett's fingers,
the coat racks, your coat, my coat, arm in arm,
your laugh in the earhole of my helmet
and what we were, we were, we were.

At the Wilco with Some Founding Fathers

Down the Havoline, Quaker State aisle
goes Jefferson, if his shirt can be believed.
The red stitching over the right pocket
proclaims this man to be a namesake
of the author of the Declaration of Independence
and if you can't believe a man's shirt
what are you going to believe?
Hamilton, what a strange coincidence,
doubts aloud that the cashier
cannot access the safe and Franklin,
spook me out, is eyeing the better wines
while recommending the Appalachian spring water.
It's all here—White Rain hair-styling spray, Tic Tacs,
flashlights, corn chips, and nation-makers.
And now Jefferson, who wanted to be remembered
for penning Virginia's statute on religious freedom,
says a standing silent prayer over a chili dog
before taking a bite and heading out
through the calibrated doors, he's nearly six feet I see,
into the republic of Friday morning.

Talc like Dust

When he finishes your cut, he sprinkles talc on a brush and sweeps your neck and ears of any stray, clipped hairs. The drift from this dusting has clouded his hand mirror, a skim of pollen on a small pond.

He gives you the mirror and swivels the big chair so that you float in the dingy, quiet waters of his shop. The light climbs down to you on its dusty ropes.

He's the last barber in town. The hair in his ears is gray and wiry. His scissors have thinned with sharpening, a flock of storks at the edge of the water.

Soon no one will drift here, drowning in the ordinary afternoon. Soon everyone will go around with the flowing, uncut hair of the dead.

Men Throwing Bricks

The one on the ground lofts two at a time
with just the right lift for them to finish
their rise as the one on the scaffold turns
to accept them like a gift and place them
on the growing stack. They chime slightly
on the catch. You'd have to do this daily,
morning and afternoon, not to marvel.

Easy Street, Continental Homes, Luck, the Destination of Southern Conversation, and Dust

Easy Street, at least *this* Easy Street, has the parking lot of the Boones Mill Pharmacy at one end and one block away it T-bones another one-lane paved pig path called Maple or Oak or something else original, and you might take this Easy Street as a short-cut if you are late for your job at the Continental Homes factory on top of the hill, which is where this was heading before it had to run a few errands and pick up something it didn't need and check out its reflection in the plate glass of Dr. Leisure's, swear to God his real name, dental office.

What this "it" is might be called a story, in the same way that fishing is called a sport, having so much to do with water temperature, and the size, color, and smell of the chosen bait, and, oh yeah, there's luck, which the people on Easy Street and at the Continental Homes factory call what happens to you, whether it's good or bad, as long as it's outside the daily sequence of events that we mostly call our lives.

Luck, for instance, is about to happen to Lonnel Mattox as he is replaying the long night's fight with his wife that began over a missing button from one of his work shirts and ended with Lonnel removing Charlene's teeth from his shoulder by jerking backwards on his handful of her hair. She removed some of the meat from his shoulder and Lonnel is reminded of this every time he swings the circular saw across the long piece of molding he is turning into shorter pieces of molding, which makes him think about the fight and he tries to retrace the angry path they took to get from a button to her throwing a pork chop to slapping and screaming and then today's piece of luck shows up as the circular saw finds his work glove and jerks his hand and *ping* the end of his index finger is on the floor still in the tip of the glove like a pinto bean in a thimble and that will be referred to throughout the factory as bad luck.

Now, I have not gotten where I started but this country would never have been stolen by people who see a forest as a shipment of mobile homes if we ever actually wound up where we intended. "The typical southern conversation is not going anywhere," the poet and professor Allen Tate wrote, so I guess he should know though I wonder what Dr. Tate would have made of the shouts and hoots and whistles that are employed, if I might be allowed to strut a little, to get over the scream of the rip, jig, circular, and table saws. I wonder if Dr. Tate ever had to wait until break time to ask a man a simple question. How can you not be going somewhere? Like the man said to the farmer, when the farmer woke him and asked how he and his car got into the farmer's alfalfa field: "Well, I was aiming for home but this is where my aim went a little wide."

"Wide Load" is their banner when they take to the interstates, hitched to a semi: half a house, the cut-away side covered with plastic sheeting, opaquing the half rooms. Now you tell me if it's not a certain kind of American genius that we can take our homes on the road, open to view, like a TV show, a set for a low-budget soap opera, rolling out of Boones Mill and heading up the Shenandoah Valley, who knows, maybe for Gettysburg, where our great-great-grandfathers, North and South, got together to make reeking heaps of meat out of each other, a regular picnic of slaughter, but that's all over now and confined to school books where it will be safe from the minds of American youth, the sons and daughters of the workers of the Continental Homes Company. There's not enough left of John Brown to molder or any other damn thing and what we have here is enterprise, the rooms ready to be joined to contain the canned applause of game shows and the Tuesday night missing button/pork chop fights.

I'm having a little trouble here. You may have noticed. It's the noise of the place. You wind up just having to watch. One woman keeps a pencil stub behind her left ear, and I still don't know why. One guy goes out to his car at lunch every day and eats behind the wheel. Every day. In the afternoon the dust of the parking lot follows you only as far as the railroad tracks. No matter how much you use the air hoses and brush off, fine dust, fine as flour, fine as lilac talc, collects in your pockets, in the wrinkles around your eyes, in the scollops of your ears. A sweet dust from the lives of trees, it's your destination, if you're lucky.

Dominion

We called them the Bible Couple,
because they had one,
a spiffy leather-bound number with its own latch
that snapped front cover to back
as though the gospel were a snake
that had to be secured in its carrying box.
They brought it everyday with their towels, umbrella, suntan lotion,
and little cooler of six Mountain Dews.

Here's their drill. After they'd get the umbrella and towels set,
they'd read the Bible together, on their stomachs, side by side,
with the intensity of Boy Scouts scouring a porno novel by flashlight.
Then they'd sit up, hold hands, and pray for 10, maybe 15 minutes.
Then they'd neck, his tongue searching her mouth
as if it were looking for words to offer God.
After a while they'd go for a swim. Actually not a swim.
They'd go in up to their chests and hug while the waves
made them bob like buoys marking baited traps.
I'm thinking only people who aren't screwing
kiss like that, that long, that hungrily, in public.
Was it faith or fear of banishment,
an angry congregation learning what they did on summer vacation,
that keeps them so starved for each other?

On our sixth day, a thunderstorm drove us in and from my porch
I could see Adam and Eve locked up on a porch across the street.
Our ark leaked.
Rain worked through the tarpaper,
and while they spoke in tongues,
it drummed on the curved Styrofoam belly
of a dropped boogie board.

Oscillating Fan

A relic from the time before AC,
when the heat, even in the dark,
was something nearly visible.

It is making a slow "No."
At one extreme the months are rifled.
Enter, orange and yellow October.

It pans and
the pages are turned in the Bible
left out after the morning devotional.

This thing has a certain passage in mind,
a sentry, checking first the days
and then Deuteronomy.

On the one hand, there's Pilate.
On the other, it's Christmas.
The months preen, adjust their feathers.

The leaves seem to regret their turning.
David, Solomon, September,
the date oil and arrival of the swallows.

Now hurricane season begins
and Pharaoh's army is swept away.
The breeze thumbs up the gospel

and then gets back to a Thursday in June,
creeks loud with runoff, sudden sky,
the light just now let be.

The Small-Town Voice of God

Band boosters man the cocoa cups.
There's a handful of steam for anyone
with a quarter, whipped cream

for another nickel. A moment
of silence, blank to fill in,
or not, the rehearsed separation

of brass and woodwinds
at the fifty. Friday night stalls.
We believe we will win

and the scoreboard exclaims
0, 0. It's a coin toss,
heads butting tails in the dirt.

Everyone's here, so that beyond
the banks of lights no one
hears the cheer go up.

After Ice and Snow

The trees have
crystal fingers.
Do they want

something warm
to hold? One
has a cardinal

like a Valentine
heart caught
in its bony grip.

Does the bird
burn those stiff
cold digits?

Now it seems
the icy tree
makes a toss,

a crimson smack,
a splash of feathers
against the pane.

Wasn't that cruel,
unnecessary? Neck
broken, it's a welt

on the ground.
On snow its red
is redder still.

Baptist

The river locks up for the night,
its movable rooms stall like boxcars.

The river's metaphor is frozen,
and now even the most unbelieving can walk

that cold pavement dusty with snow.
They used to saw it up,

great slabs of river stored
in sawdust beneath the houses.

"One winter we hauled off half the river"
goes one of their gospels, a common testament

retold on the river bank when the water blackens
back into moving, when to cool off

you go in and under, quiet,
oh it's quiet, in its rushing.

The Wedding at Cana

The bride and the bridegroom
have not heard the words.
"Will there be enough at the reception?"
The mother of the bride, the father
of the groom, even the minister,
because he reads them at every wedding,
have not heard the words.
But the six stone jars have heard them again.

Now it seems like years since the ceremony.
See the flush in the faces of all gathered,
the body heat, the sweetness
of the flowers strapped
to the bridesmaids' wrists. This is the wine
with the warmth in it, the last glasses,
the little too much, the giddiness,
the stirring in the loins,
the miraculous sip that contains the curve
of that one's breast, this one's back and dark eyes,
her slender hands, his hair thick and rich as fur.
Have another.
The hour has come for the bride and groom to leave
and in the modern fashion seeds are thrown.
The birds, the small, feathered vessels,
will know what to do, will take the seeds to the treetops,
and beyond the treetops, even unto the heavens.

Out Here

Where Rogers intersects Eubanks,
just down from the county dump,
the plastic anatomical model of a heart
is broken on the road side.

Eubanks. The "E" capital and silent.

It's only a model, this broken heart,
the veins plump with blood-red polymers.

Eubanks. Pronounced, of course, U-banks.
The visible is tricky business.

It must have fallen off a truck from the high school,
discarded when the new models arrived for Advanced Biology.

On the road beside the heart a four-foot black snake
has been thoroughly crushed
into an emblem of itself,
infinity, a Greek letter,
which is it?
A beagle sniffs whatever scent is left,
now he rolls on it.
A slight scent, silent and pungent, will do.

It's all beneath a blood-red sign
that reads STOP.
Of course, no one does,
out here, no traffic, the glitter
of skin unpronounceable on the macadam.

Digging

I'm digging a drainage ditch beside my house.
Tomorrow I will feel the length of it in my shoulders and back.
I will enjoy thinking "heft" and "mattock,"
those flinty *T*s a pleasure
in the silent language of thinking
when the ditch is complete.
Roots snag the blade, and to free the mattock
I work the handle like a lever,
like the start/stop stick on old-fashioned carousels.
And now the mothers and fathers have stepped off
the ride's platform and the children are going around
on their gaudy animals with the open red mouths.
Some are crying, some are not.
I smell fresh-turned dirt.
Sparks fly from struck quartz.
The word is *chert.*
I notice shards, like shrapnel, have cut
my bare chest and there are flecks of blood.
This red wound in the dirt has leapt up.

Getting Turned Around in Point Pleasant Where the Kanawha and Ohio Rivers Converge

First I was in Ohio,
then West Virginia.

Another wrong turn
and then Ohio again.

How could I get so confused
in such a small town

though small townness
is certainly no bar to confusion?

How do you say the name
of this river, I asked

a man who looked like he knew
where he was. "O-Hi-O"

he said deliberately.
No, the other river, I said.

"Do you think it is
Can-A-Wa-Ha?" he said.

Both rivers were calm
and workable as mules,

though only one provided
the border for the states.

I went back and forth
across their broad backs.

O-Wa-O. They glittered
in the sun that day

as I went over and back,
as I changed states.

The other side was other
until I arrived there,

but it was Pleasant
at least half the time,

and death rode along
with me as always

but I didn't notice,
singing, changing, not

having to bother with tolls,
released to go by the light.

Where We Go When We Die

She insisted I take a "slip"
when I admired the purple
Chinese lantern-like blossoms.
It's unruly stuff, crawling
to every limb that it can reach.
Its tendrils snake across
open air, green filaments
that catch nearby branches
and then begin their binding.
The pines and even oaks around
her place were choked with it,
the vines muscling up over years
to cords that squeezed the trunks.
It was a kind of death, this life,
this hardy latching on.
So I was vigilant, I snipped
each thin line it cast.
The moccasin runners it sent
through the leaf litter
I hacked loose and tore from the ground.
Maybe that's why the bush
I did allow refused to bloom.
It bore only slim leaves,
no lacy clusters in the spring,
until this spring, the first
without her hold upon the earth.

Live

Just a moment ago
the morning stopped.
You know how it does that
some mornings, the kids,
slouched on the buses,
already hauled off to school
and the commuters gone
with their blue puff
of tailpipe smoke
and not yet the hour
for the trash truck.
All the news in the paper
is an hour old.
That's when it happens.
The sun stalls
and you're sure
it will stay,
varnishing the deck
with its light
just this way forever.
And it does
until the wren
starts singing
its little earthly song,
its caught-in-time song
from the perishing throat.
That live feathered pipe
trills and trips the morning
back into its going on.

From Whence

Tonight, the moon is hauling bituminous,
two hundred cars.
When it hits the trestle you'll hear the deck timbers rattle.
Cinder chips spike the black roundabout.
This is the dead light, just bright enough
to make a shadow if you're out in the dark.
The moon has the throttle and the all clear.
The moon is on government business
and the rails are empty all the way up the valley.
This is light enough to read a short note by.
Tonight, the moon's got papers and two pushers.
It's highballing combustible rock to a fare-thee-well.
Head lamp rocking from the soft roadbed,
this is light with a load.
This is light there's no stopping.
This is dug-up light, light from all the graves
when the graves give off light.
This is light with wheels.
Come shine, silver me a while.